ASK ISAAC ASIMOV ?

Why does the Moon change shape?

Heinemann

First published in Great Britain by Heinemann Library
an imprint of Heinemann Publishers (Oxford) Ltd
Halley Court, Jordan Hill, Oxford OX2 8EJ

OXFORD LONDON EDINBURGH MADRID
ATHENS BOLOGNA PARIS MELBOURNE
SYDNEY AUCKLAND SINGAPORE TOKYO
IBADAN NAIROBI HARARE GABORONE
PORTSMOUTH NH (USA)

98 97 96 95 94

10 9 8 7 6 5 4 3 2 1

British Library Cataloguing in Publication Data is available from the British Library on request.

ISBN 0 431 07654 5

Cover designed and pages typeset by Philip Parkhouse
Printed in China

Picture Credits
pp. 2-3, National Optical Astronomy Observatories; pp. 4-5, Frank Zullo, © 1989; pp. 6-7, Julian Baum; pp. 8-9, Regis Lefebure/Third Coast, © 1990; p. 9 (inset), Keith Ward; pp. 10-11, Hale Observatories; pp. 10-11 (background), National Optical Astronomy Observatories; pp. 12-13, Keith Ward; p. 14, © Gareth Stevens, Inc.; p. 15, © Tom Miller; p. 16 (inset), © Gareth Stevens, Inc.; pp. 16-17, © William P. Sterne, Jr.; p. 18, Frank Zullo, © 1985; p. 19, courtesy of NASA; p. 21, Bishop Museum; pp. 22-24, Rick Karpinski/DeWalt and Associates

Cover photograph © Science Photo Library/Keith Kent
Back cover photograph © Sygma/D. Kirkland

Series editor: Elizabeth Kaplan
Series designer: Sabine Huschke
Picture researcher: Daniel Helminak
Assistant picture researcher: Diane Laska
Consulting editor: Matthew Groshek

Contents

A world of questions 4
Why does the Moon shine brightly? 6
The Moon's changing faces 9
What are the Moon's phases called? 10
When does the Moon wax and wane? 13
Why does the Moon change shape? 14
Now you see it, now you don't 16
Which planets appear to change shape? .. 18
What is a lunar calendar? 20
Ruler of the night sky 22

Glossary 23
Index 24

Words that appear in the glossary are printed in **bold** the first time they occur in the text.

A world of questions

Our world is full of strange and beautiful things. The night sky glimmers with stars. Lightning branches from huge clouds during a thunderstorm. Sometimes we have questions about the things we see around us. Asking questions helps us appreciate the many wonders of the universe.

For instance, have you noticed that the **Moon** changes shape from one night to the next? Sometimes it's a beautiful circle of light. Sometimes it's only half a circle. Sometimes it's just a sliver. Why does this happen? Let's find out.

Why does the Moon shine brightly?

The Moon is a round, rocky world. It has tall mountains and deep **craters**. We can see these features because the Sun shines its light on the Moon.

The Moon does not produce its own light. It appears to shine because of the sunlight bouncing off its surface. This light is **reflected** back to Earth as moonlight. The Moon's silvery light sparkling on a field of snow makes winter nights seem lonely and mysterious. The glow of the **harvest Moon** makes autumn nights seem soft and warm.

Sun

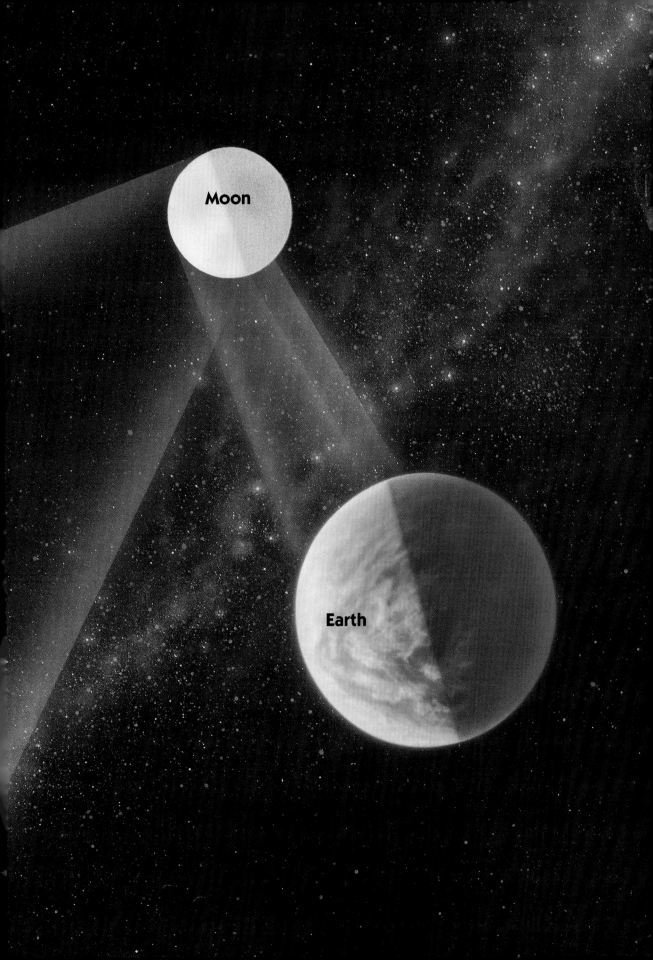

The Moon's changing faces

Although the Moon is a **sphere**, it does not always look like one. In fact, it seems to change shape every night. Sometimes you might see the Moon as a round orange ball rising in the sky. Sometimes you might see it as a silver wedge among the stars. You might notice it as a pockmarked half circle, hanging in the sky during the day, or you might not be able to find the Moon at all. We call these different shapes of the Moon its **phases**.

What are the Moon's phases called?

The phases of the Moon have different names. When the Moon looks like a round ball, it is called a full Moon. When it is just a sliver, we call it a crescent Moon.

full Moon

crescent Moon

When the Moon appears as a half-circle wedge, we call it a half Moon. When the Moon is between half and full, it is called a gibbous Moon. The thinnest crescent Moon is called a new Moon.

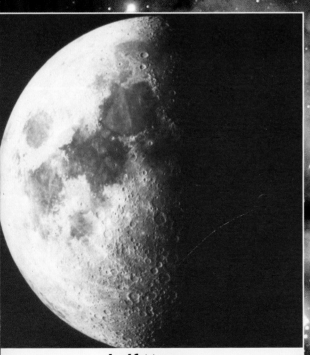

half Moon

gibbous Moon

When does the Moon wax and wane?

The Moon passes through all its phases in about 29 days. Beginning as a new Moon, it grows to a crescent Moon, a half Moon, a gibbous Moon and then a full Moon. This process takes just over two weeks. During this time, we say that the Moon is **waxing**.

Over the next two weeks the full Moon shrinks. It becomes a gibbous Moon, a half Moon, a crescent and finally disappears, ready to become a new Moon again. During this time we say that the Moon is **waning**. The picture shows some of the Moon's phases as it waxes and wanes.

Why does the Moon change shape?

If you shine a light on a round object, such as a ball, half the ball will be in light and half will be in shadow. The same thing happens when the Sun shines on the Moon.

14

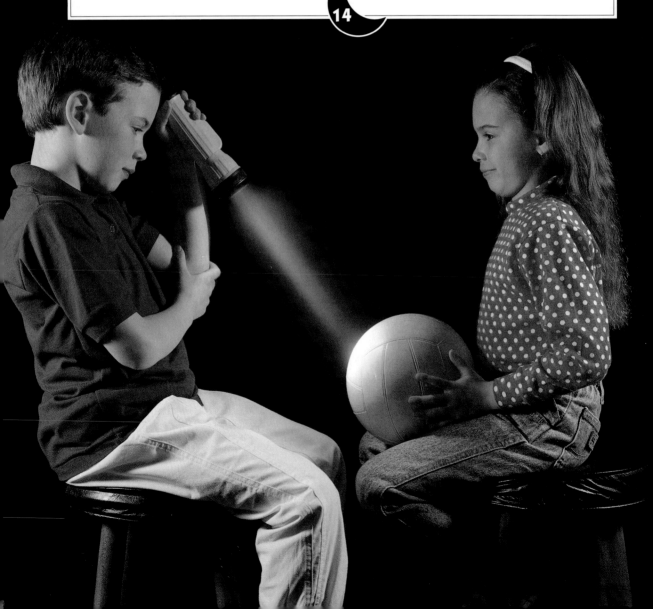

Seen from space, the Moon is always half in sunlight and half in shadow. The outer ring of the diagram below shows this. The inner ring shows how the Moon looks from Earth. During a full Moon, we see the entire face of the Moon lit by the Sun. Before a new Moon, the side of the Moon facing us is entirely in shadow. Between these times, we see different amounts of the Moon's face lit up. This is why the Moon changes shape.

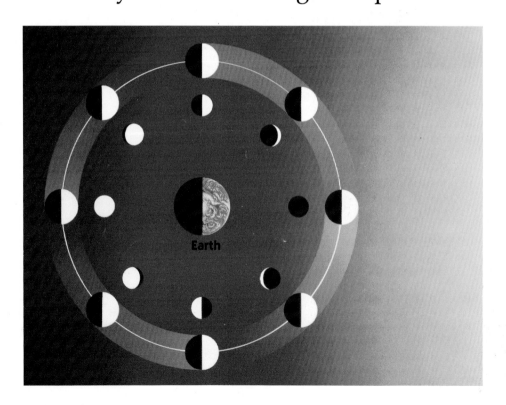

Now you see it, now you don't

Many calendars show dates when the Moon will be in different phases. But, on any given night, you may have to check the sky at different times to find the Moon. Sometimes the Moon rises early in the evening. At other times, it rises later at night.

The picture opposite shows the crescent Moon and the planet **Venus** setting over a city. The photographer took the picture over several hours. During that time, the Moon and Venus sank lower and lower in the sky.

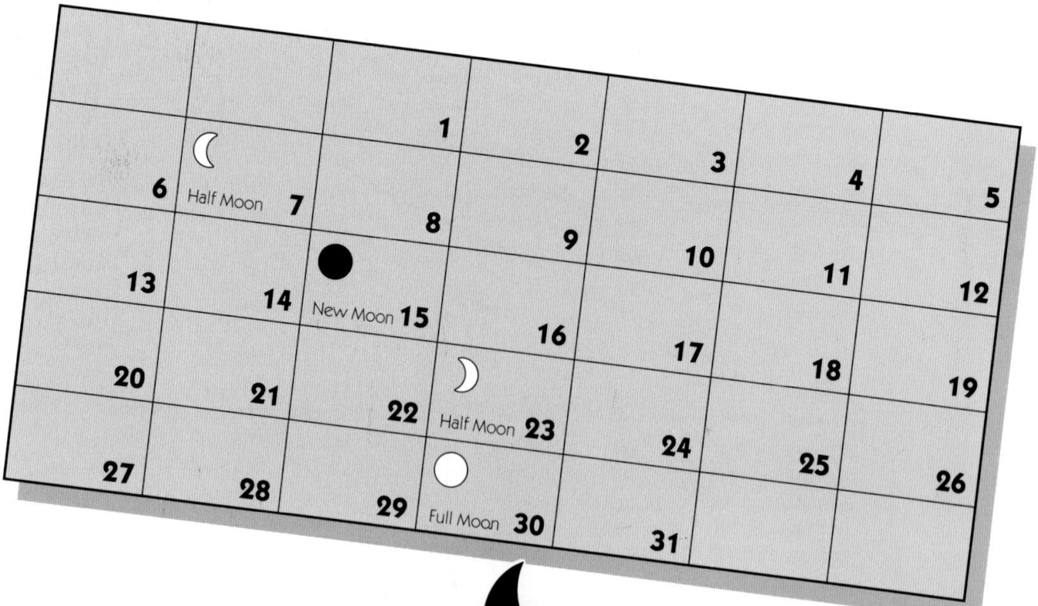

		☾		1	2	3	4	5
6	Half Moon 7		8		9	10	11	12
13	14	⬤ New Moon 15		16	17	18	19
20	21	22	☽ Half Moon 23		24	25	26
27	28	29	◯ Full Moon 30	31		

Which planets appear to change shape?

The Moon is not the only **heavenly body** that seems to change shape when viewed from Earth. **Mercury**, shown right, and Venus also go through phases. These planets sometimes pass between the Earth and the Sun. For this reason, we see different amounts of their surfaces lit up when they are at different points in their orbits.

Sometimes Mercury and Venus look like full circles of light. Other times, they appear as crescents. But you can only see the phases if you view these planets through a telescope.

What is a lunar calendar?

People sometimes use calendars based on the phases of the Moon. Such calendars are called lunar calendars. In a lunar calendar, the new Moon makes the beginning of each month. Most years have twelve months, but some years have thirteen months. Adding an extra month keeps lunar calendars in step with the seasons. The Hebrew calendar and the Islamic calendar are lunar calendars. The names of the months in the Islamic calendar are shown around the edges of these pages.

Islamic astronomers, such as those shown on the right, kept a close watch on the Moon and other heavenly bodies to make sure their calendars remained accurate.

The calendar commonly used today is based on the seasons, not on the phases of the Moon. But the divisions of the calendar are still called months, after the Moon.

Ruler of the night sky

The Moon has always been an object of beauty and wonder. Today we know more about the Moon than ever before. Many spacecraft have flown past it, and astronauts have jumped around on its surface. But the Moon still holds charm and mystery for us whenever we gaze at its changing face.

Glossary

crater: a hole on a planet or moon that forms when a meteorite strikes it or when a volcano explodes

harvest Moon: the full Moon that occurs nearest to September 21

heavenly body: any star, planet, natural satellite or other natural object that is found in space

Mercury: the planet nearest to the Sun

Moon: the heavenly body that circles Earth

phase: a change that usually occurs as part of a cycle, such as the changing faces of the Moon

reflect: to bounce back; light reflects off the Moon's surface and travels to Earth

sphere: an object that is round like a ball

Venus: the second planet from the Sun; Venus is the planet closest to the Earth

wane: to grow smaller or shrink; the Moon wanes when it goes from a full Moon to darkness

wax: to grow larger; the Moon waxes when it goes from a new Moon to a full Moon

Index

calendars 16, 20
craters 6, 23
crescent Moon 10, 13,
  16–17

Earth 6, 15, 18, 23

full Moon 11, 13

gibbous Moon 11, 13

half Moon 11, 13
harvest Moon 6, 23

light 6, 14, 18, 23

Mercury 18, 23
months 20
moonlight 6

new Moon 11, 13, 15,
  20, 23

phases
  of Mercury 18
  of the Moon 4, 8–17
  of Venus 18

shadows 14, 15
stars 4, 9, 23
Sun 6, 14, 15, 18, 23
sunlight 6, 15
surface of the Moon 6, 23

telescope 18

universe 4

Venus 16, 18, 23

waning 13, 23
waxing 13, 23